Tristan da Cunha

Naira Matevosyan

From "Phineus, the piglet, likes to travel" series

Copyright © 2017, L'Auteur Librairie, ISBN: 978-1542392310

Contents

The Flag

Commuting - 4

Profile - 10

Accommodation - 22

Flora and fauna - 25

Things to do - 30

Things not to do - 38

Things to eat and to drink - 40

Healthcare - 43

Education - 45

Crime - 47

Packing back - 48

The Coat of Arms

"If isolation tempers the strong, it is the stumbling-block of the uncertain." ~ Paul Cezanne.

Hi again! I am ~~Phynee~~ Phineus, a solitary ~~trou~~ globetrotter and a ~~voca~~ vacationer on the budget.

Paul Cezanne, The Bay of L'Estaque

The elfin list of my destinations includes uncharted countries and territories, where I can achieve the tranquil deportment I am craving for, that equanimity far-flung from the everyday routine - something I thoroughly try to refine.

While I don't care about geopolitics or info-wars, I do care much of what Cezanne has said. .... a place of complete isolation that would "~~stumble-block the very uncertain.~~"

I forage to find such a place, as what's certain in our lives is quite what pushes us away from it.

As William Congreve suggests, "Uncertainty and expectation are the joys of life."

Hanging from the perspective, I am heading the most isolated country in the world. Follow me, I'm NOT kidding!

Commuting

Last time I was visiting Palau and I must confess, commuting was rather uncomplicated. The most remote inhabited archipelago in the world, Tristan da Cunha can be reached with the help of two mandatory things: (1) courage and (2) personal boat. This country is not everyone's cup of tea. Commuting to this place is even harder than to reach to the Faroe Islands (Denmark).

If you're familiar with Jule Verne's novel, "The Sphinx of the Ice Fields" (1897), that sphinx referred to Tristan da Cunha. It's not surprising that Zinnie Harris has named this place "Further than the Furthest Thing" in her homonymous play (2000).

The remote location of these islands makes the commuting an absolute challenge. Lacking an airport, Tristan can be reached only by sea. Fishing boats from South Africa service the islands only 8-9 times a year. The RMS Saint Helena used to connect the main island (Slotenhoff) to South Africa once each year during its January voyage, but has done so only twice in the last few years: in 2006 and 2011.

Following the given five-year pattern, one would expect another "Helena-voyage" in 2016. Yet, it wasn't so. There is no direct, regular service to Tristan da Cunha from South Africa.

For more details on how to reach St. Helena itself, visit the jaguars' tour-book (ISBN: 978-1511519076).

The harbor at Edinburgh of the Seven Seas known as Calshot Harbour, is named after the place in Hampshire where the islanders temporarily stayed during the volcanic eruption.

Calshot is where you gonna anchor your boat inshore.

But before you beach your boat, nudge the bottom, and hitch the two sea-knots at the shore of Tristan, you first need to commute to South Africa.

For another Helena (Montana) piglet like myself, the courageous trip - in seek of uncertainty - starts from the HLN (Helena Regional). I am taking an economy flight to Cape Town, South Africa.

The cheapest coach with a short notice and in the high season costs about US $3,100. Flights of this schedule last 55-60 hours including the two mandatory stops in Seattle (Tacoma Intl.) and London (Heathrow), with Alaska Airlines and British Airways as the common carriers.

Reaching Edinburgh of the Seven Seas (Tristan da Cunha) from Cape Town (South Africa) requires a thorough planning ahead. It takes five to six days to draw the 2810-kilometer nautical-line in between. The South African polar research ship, SA Agulhas, and the fishing vessels, Edinburgh and Baltic Trader, set sail between Cape Town and Tristan da Cunha several times a year, every year.

   A return ticket aboard Agulhas is about US $ 1,300 and on the fishing vessels is US $ 800. There is no fee for children under 6 years of age.

   Below is the list of Edinburgh's research shipping schedules from- and to- Tristan, for 2017:

   From Cape to Tristan – Jan. 14, Mar. 18, May 6, June 22
   From Tristan to Cape- Jan. 21, Mar. 25, May 13, June 29

   The fishing schedule for Edinburgh as follows:

   From Cape to Tristan – Mar. 01, May 24, July 10
   From Tristan to Cape- Feb. 23, May 18, July 04.

Visit http://www.tristandc.com/shipping.php for more details on shipping schedules.

In summary, the one way journey from Montana to Tristan costs in the neighborhood of USD $ 3,800. Unless I have a private boat, in the last portion of this trip I have to rely on the scarce schedule of S.A. Agulhas or Edinburgh. Being super rich and having a personal jet is not a solution either, as there is no airstrip and no airport on Tristan da Cunha.

Having all this fathomed, next question is whether after such a taxing journey I would be granted a permission to cross the border?

And the answer is affirmative!
Tristan is a British dependency, just like the islands of St. Helena or Ascension. An Entry Permit costs GBP £17 and allows a stay of up to 183 days. You will need to provide evidence of a return ticket or funds for it, health insurance, adequate accommodation and sufficient funds for the stay. It goes without saying, that your passport must be valid for the proposed duration of the stay.

For a stay longer than 183 days, you should apply to the St Helena Immigration Control Board, or Tristan's Administrator Council and have a landing stamp in your passport. Email at enquiriestdc1@gmail.com and specify the date and purpose of your visit, and the address where you will stay. Landing stamps are also issued to passengers and crew who do not intend to go ashore, but rather wish to have their travel endorsed as a stamped memoir.

9

Profile

☼ Tristan da Cunha is an archipelago of fairly small islands in the middle of South Atlantic. It is composed of four islands: Gough, Inaccessible, Nightingale, and Tristan itself. A British territory, it officially is administered by the government of St. Helena, another fully autonomous British island situated 2430 kilometers to the north.

Tristan da Cunha is the most remote inhabited island in the world - 2800 kilometers away from the nearest continent,

Africa.

Tristan's entire population is roughly 300 people, concentrated on the only flat bit of this volcanic landmass, the hamlet of Edinburgh of the Seven Seas on the main island. All other islands in the archipelago, are uninhabited: Inaccessible Island, Nightingale Island, Middle Island, and Stoltenhoff Island.

Established in the early 19th century, Edinburgh of the Seven Seas village is located on the north coast and is home to

12

70 families, all of whom are farmers.

Electricity is supplied by diesel generators. The island's lone road - a narrow, winding path - is flanked by bungalow-style cottages, potato patches and roaming cows. The looming volcanic cliffs and low-lying mist create a secluded, hazy setting.

Gough Island, some 300km away, hosts a weather and scientific research outpost.

Hmm... I see you're judging me. But before you'd scoff at my plan and its cost, think it this way: you always have the option to view the most remote inhabited soil online. Yet, walking on it, on the earth's very end grabbed with the cobalt waves of Atlantic, is completely a different feel. To have it, I am paying about $4,500.

I want to be physically present in the clime to understand how it could happen, that there is a country with GDP per capitum of $5,622 (8 times lower than that in the UK, and 11 times lower than that in the US), unemployment rate of 14% (5 times higher than the UK's and 3 times higher than the US's), and is featured with life expectancy of 79.5 years (UK's is 81.5 and US's is 78.7) and maternal mortality rate of 1.9 (against UK's 9.02 and US's 21.3) in the same cross section of 2015.

Is that the positive impact of isolation or a statistical bias?

Whatever it is, the Tristanians love their land, a peaceful, pared-back existence with few anxieties, unless the volcano erupts.

Such was the case in 1961, when earthquakes, landslides, and an eruption from one of the north vents sent the entire population to England via Cape Town. Fed up with England's busy streets and savage winters, most returned two years after to embrace their all-cleared from the geologists land.

Now that the volcano has calmed down, life on Tristan da Cunha is an exercise in patience and planning!

This mysterious archipelago was first sighted in 1506 by a Portuguese explorer, Tristão da Cunha. The rough seas prevented him landing; yet, he named the main island after his name. The first full survey of the islands was made in 1767 by crew of the French corvette, Heure du Berger.

The first permanent settler was Jonathan Lambert, from Salem, Massachusetts, who landed in 1810. In 1816, the United Kingdom annexed the islands, ruling them from the Cape Colony in South Africa. Such a measure was taken to ensure that the French would not rescue Napoleon Bonaparte from the prison in Saint Helena, as well as to prevent the United States from using again Tristan a cruiser base.

The islands were occupied by a garrison of British Marines and the civilian population gradually grew. Whalers set up bases on the islands for operations in Southern Atlantic. However, the opening of the Suez Canal in 1869, together with the gradual transition from sailing ships to coal-fired steam ships, increased the isolation of the islands. The ships no longer needed to port at Tristan, for lengthy sail from Europe to East Asia.

In 1867, Prince Alfred, Duke of Edinburgh and second son of Queen Victoria, visited the islands. The main settlement, Edinburgh of the Seven Seas, was named in honor of his visit.

On 12 January 1938, Britain declared the dependency of Saint Helena, establishing the British Overseas Territory of Saint Helena and Dependencies, which also included nearby Ascension Island.

During World War Two, Britain used Tristan da Cunha as a secret Royal Navy weather and radio station coded as HMS Atlantic Isle, to monitor Nazi U-boats (which were required to maintain radio contact) and shipping movements in the South Atlantic Ocean.

Today, Tristan is a British Overseas Territory, with Queen Elizabeth II as the Head of State. The current Governor is Lisa Phillips, formerly the Head of Department of International Development in Kenya, and the acting administrator is Ian Lavarello, the "Chief Islander."

It may erroneously seem, that the Queen's role is symbolic, just cutting the ribbons in certain celebrations. Yet, it's not so.

The Queen posses a total power. She is the one who may announce emergencies, appoint or dismiss Governors or Chief Islanders, pardon criminals, or give military orders. The anthem of Tristan is "God Save the Queen." Thus, the islanders swear allegiance not to the people or the flag, but rather to the Queen.

Tristan no longer uses the local St. Helena Pound as its currency. Instead, it uses the British Pound Sterling.

The islands' unique social - economic organization is based on the principles set forth by William Glass in 1817, when the latter established a settlement based on equality.

Export earnings generate from the commercial crawfish, the Tristan rock lobster (Jasus tristani) industry which is symbolized in Tristan's Coat of Arms (see page 1).

In addition to farming as a major revenue infrastructure, the locals sustain themselves by selling souvenirs, handcrafts, rare postal stamps, coins and of course, the famous Tristanian "love socks."

The religious freedom in the islands brings together Protestants who form the majority (75.9%) of residents, as well as Baptists 2.1%, Seventh Day Adventists 1.8%, Salvation Army 1.7%, New Apostolic 1.4%), Jehovah's Witnesses 4.1%, Roman Catholics 1.2%, other 2.5%, and atheists 6.1%.

Gough Island was first known as Diego Alvarez, until it was sighted in 1721 by Captain Gough, from his ship Richmond. This brought a new name. Although Gough Island is a UK territory, the only permanent settlement is South African. This island has no sheltered harbor or anchorage. The only suitable landing place for boats is at Glen Anchorage in Quest Bay on the east coast.

SA Agulhas departs from Cape Town to Tristan da Cunha then onward to Gough on the annual relief voyage.

Getting around Gough comes with great difficulty - combination of excessively steep terrain and incredibly dense vegetation - and no paths to speak of. There are no public accommodations on Gough Island as well. Yet, this island is a UNSECO World Heritage site

The island hosts the only postal office of Tristan as well as the South Atlantic Ocean meteorological station.

Note, there is <u>no</u> mobile phone coverage in all islands. Since 1998, there was an Internet service but its high cost made it almost impractical and the locals used it solely to send email. The connection was extremely unreliable, a 64 KB/sec satellite phone connection provided by Inmarsat. From 2006, a very-small-aperture terminal provides 3072 kbit/s of publicly accessible bandwidth via an internet cafe.

Hydroacoustic Station, the main Island

Post Office, island Gough

Here, you can order authentic postal stamps and cards with your name and date of visit as well as drop your mail in the red pillar box outside the office.

Accommodation

While booking bed-and-breakfast in Tristan da Cunha, forget expedia.com, orbitz.com, hotels.com, or travelocity.com. There are no flights to, and no standard hotels in the archipelago.

Accommodation in Tristan comes with a range of government-issued and private options (cottages, bungalows). Booking information is provided in http://www.tristandc.com

There are six guest houses available on a catered or self-catered basis. Catered prices are in line with full board home stays, and self catered prices are £25 plus utility charges.

The fee for children under 12 years is £12.50, and for younger than 2years - £2.50. The privately owned guest houses charge the 75% of the rental fee, as the remaining 25% is paid to the Government. Here we go! I got a "supermarket" neighbor.

Tristan Tourism Department offers its unique properties for overnight stays (page 24). Isolated behind the Big Watron, this accommodation promises a singular experience for those braves who are determined for the unknown feelings and tastes.

William Glass guest house

Rockhopper cottage

Sea View Lodge

Flora and Fauna

Tristan is primarily known for its wildlife. Many species have broad circumpolar distribution in the South Atlantic and South Pacific. Thus, many that occur in Tristan da Cunha can be found in New Zealand. An example is Nertera depressa.

Nertera Depressa

Some 53 species of flowering plants as well as 38 ferns and club mosses are endemic to the islands. There are three zones, depending on the altitudes. (I) The coastal fringes are covered by large tussock-forming grasses, like Spartina arundinacea in Nightingale Island, and Poa flabellata in Gough island (page 26). (II) Above the tussock grasslands follows a zone where salt-spray influence is small, and nutrient input by birds is relatively low, with a mosaic of Phylica arborea woodland and fernbrake communities. (III) The lower zone is completely overgrown by alien species, notably by Yorkshire fog and sheep's sorrel (page 26).

Spartina arundinacea

Poa flabellata

Phylica arborea

South Atlantic albatross

26

Moorhen

The endemic birds are slightly smaller and duller than those on Nightingale and Inaccessible islands. In 1956 eight Gough moorhens were released at Sandy Point on Tristan, and have subsequently colonized the island

There is a colony of Northern Rockhopper penguins (pinnamins) at the east end of Sandy Point. The penguins come onshore to breed between August and December, and again for moulting between January and March.

Rockhopper penguin

Harvesting penguin eggs is a tradition on Tristan. Since the northern Rockhopper is listed as an endangered species, its eggs collection is prohibited.

Various species of whales and dolphins can be seen around Tristan from time to time.

The subantarctic fur seal (Arctocephalus tropicalis) can be found in Tristan archipelago, mostly on Gough Island.

Fur seal

The Tristan albatross and Atlantic petrel are also native to the islands of Tristan.

Since farming was established in the archipelago, the predominant cattle is the sheep.

Tristan albatross

28

Atlantic petrel

    Tristan's steep mountain slopes are ideal for sheep who thrive particularly on the lush pastures of the mountain base. There are over 600 Tristan mountain sheep.
    The summer season gets underway with Sheep Shearing Day held on a Saturday in mid-December. Almost the entire population gathers on the far end of Patches Plain where the sheep pens are sited. Hand-clippers are used in the shearing and the wool is later carded, spun and hand-knitted into garments, some of which are sold under the name "37 Degrees South Knitwear Range." Also, stuffed roasted mutton is Tristan's favorite Christmas dish.

Things to do

Once we sorted out all "residents" of Tristan da Cunha, it's time to roam and meet them in flesh!

But before exposing myself to the wilderness of the west Oceania, I need to pause and repeat under my snout: "Phineus! There are no restaurants, no hotels in Tristan. Credit cards are not accepted, the beaches aren't safe for swimming, and every month brings some 17 - 26 days of heavy rainfall. Smack-dab in the middle of the island lies a giant volcano. And most importantly..."

I don't care! What I came to see and to feel is how Tristan da Cunha is enticing, as it offers something that no other destination can <u>ever do</u>: the most extreme isolation!

Even in this refuge from the world, there is a range of activities to consider (excursions, hiking, fishing, climbing, golfing) - using experienced Islanders as guides.

Due to rugged, steep terrain, going all the way around the island is difficult, but if just staying in the Settlement on Tristan, the flat, grassy ground is easy to manage.

There is a paved road (M1) from Edinburgh of the Seven Seas (aka the Settlement) to the Potato Patches - which are about 3 miles away. Local transport is available to the Potato Patches. It could be an islander's car or tractor.

A public bus service is available in the mornings. The pensioners can ride the bus for free. For all other adults, the charge is £5 upon return. Note, you cannot rent a vehicle on the island. So, you gonna rely on your feet and spirit! For that, you must eat well, sleep well, dream well, and breathe deeply.

A Montana piglet, the first thing I'd wish to do is to head the Potato Patches. Those form a series of rectilinear walled fields, normally without gates, where potatoes and other vegetables have been grown for over 150 years. The tiny fields offer shelter from gale force winds on this exposed part of the island. Every island family owns and cultivates several patches and all help to plant, tend and harvest crops (page 33).

So, my nest legitimate question is: "did I spend about $4.5K to visit Tristan to check with their progress with potato

The Potato Patches, main island

Potato Patches

planting and harvesting?"
And the answer is negative. I came to Tristan for another serious reason: to have a ride on their public bus.

Relax! I am kidding. My next stop would be Burntwood and the Peak, massive 1000 - meter high former sea cliffs rising behind Burntwood, the highest peaks of Tristan. These are barriers form the North-West winds. Hillpiece is a fairly young volcanic cone, the loose ash rock of which is being eroded by South Atlantic breakers. Behind Hillpiece is the island's 'main road' linking the Settlement (to northwest) with the Patches Plain (to southeast).

I am finally on the summit. Don't you worry about me. I'm not going to base-jump. I have a purpose and dream to live further. and that is... to rather base-jump from the Queen Mary's Peak, a 2062 - meter volcanic cone with a central crater (page 34). Upper

Burntwood and the Peak

33

slopes are mainly bare of vegetation and are chiefly composed of loose volcanic ash or cinders, produced during eruptions from the central crater. Heavy rain has already reduced the height of the Peak (probably by some 200 meters) by gully erosion as seen in the radial V-shaped valleys with intervening narrow ridges leading to the broader base.

Queen Mary's Peak

After my lungs are well oxygenated, my muscles are washed by adrenaline, and my thinking device starts working faster, I realize that I need to leave these peaks and visit the Sandy Point in the Lee, eastern coast of the main island. A relatively wide black sand beach, it is fringed by low cliffs and a narrow sloping shelf extending up to the lowest of Tristan's fringing hills. Here, a farm was set up in the 1950s but attempts to cultivate vegetables failed. Still, the pine plantation and fruit trees of apple, pear, and plum make this area attractive.

Sandy Point, The Lee

My next stop is Gough island, a UNESCO world heritage site. There I will visit the famous caves, the Meteorological Center, and of course, the Calshot Harbor (page 36).

Gough island

Where else, if not in Gough, one can observe such a heartfelt friendship between the albatross and the mice! I always found the symbiotic relationship between the certain animals as mundane. But this one is simply fascinating.

I am finally in the Calshot Harbor. Don't get me wrong. I am not going to leave Tristan today. I'm here to visit the fishing factory, the large gray building overlooking the harbor (page 37), also to take

Calshot Harbor

36

advantage of the local craft ferry rides as you may see the ferries offloaded in the harbor.

The harbor is only equipped for the inshore craft, so ships must anchor offshore. It hosts ferry passengers and the cargo.

I smell fish! I divine purpose to be here! But before I'd commence to the Tristanian cuisine, I must share with you one more chapter from my diary: things to avoid in the archipelago.

Things not to do

<u>Remember:</u> Tristan da Cunha is part of the British Overseas Territory along with St Helena and Ascension. Its Administrator and Governor are British Foreign and Commonwealth Office employees and the maintenance of the governance of Tristan da Cunha is overseen on behalf of Her Majesty Queen Elizabeth II by members of the House of Lords and House of Commons/Parliament, through the Foreign Secretary and other Government colleagues.

Here, the rule of law and the security are provided by the Crown. Accordingly, when visiting Tristan you must behave as a Briton, more precisely - as an Englishman.

You <u>MUST NOT</u>:

- Visit with a passport that expires in less than 183 days;
- Visit without ample cash funds for the stay, accidents, and return;
- Visit without comprehensive health insurance;
- Visit without prior immunization for measles-mumps-rubella (MMR), diphtheria-tetanus-pertussis (DTP), varicella (chickenpox), polio, hepatitis B, rabies, and Zika virus.
- Visit without having seen your health care provider in less than 4-6 weeks prior the travel;

- Lack in protection against the insect bites;
- Share body fluids;
- Bother the albatross nests and other animals;
- Visit the summits without ample drinking water and food supply, radio-connection, and clothing layers;
- Drink tap water;
- Look for a hotel, for a restaurant, or for an ATM machine;
- Look for a museum or movie theatre;
- Complain about the country you visit, for its better to open your heart and eyes to the destination - so the destination will love and see you back.

Things to eat and to drink

The volcanic rocks of Tristan aren't known for cultivating native plants, green and root vegetables. The locals heavily rely on potatoes, a dietary staple. If you remember, the archipelago is accessible only by boat and only for 60 days a year. Those 60 days are scattered from January to December, but because of weather conditions, there are very few days between May and September when boats can dock. The islands are virtually unapproachable for five months. In addition, the half of each month is dressed with heavy rainfalls.

In life endangered with dwindling resources, the locals imprint the original settlers from 1800s, and their desire to stay on the islands is more than just a choice. These braves have to innovate and create to self-sustain.

Only one of the four islands is inhabited, with houses

grouped closely in what residents call "The Settlement," a town named after the Duke of Edinburgh's visit in 1867. Cows, chickens, duck, and geese are all raised on Tristan for food; sheep for the wool. The Rockhopper Penguins are divine, and solely for the natural entertainment and admiration.

    Reserving the idea of visiting a local home to taste a roasted mutton or butter-squash in the perspective, I am visiting now Cafe da Cunha located in the Post Office and Tourism Centre. Here, you can purchase hot and cold drinks, sandwiches, soups, and hot meals. There is also Albatross Bar, the islands only pub, open in

Roasted local, TDC lobster

Cafe da Cunha

the evenings, Monday through Saturday, and in Sunday afternoons. A range of food and drink items are also available for a few hours purchase at the Island Store.

Bar Albatross

Healthcare

Camogli Hospital, named after the home town of 1892's Italian settlers, was built on an exposed site at the west end of the Settlement near Hottentot Gulch in 1971. It replaced the original 'Station Hospital' in temporary buildings erected in 1942 when Tristan was the home of the HMS Atlantic Isle naval station. Prior to 1942, Tristan had no specialist medical services, and relied on self-help and any random aid of specialists aboard the passing ships.

Camogli Hospital, the old building

A new health centre is planned to replace Camogli Hospital and will be known as the Camogli Healthcare Centre.

The flooring of the new center has started on January 2nd, 2017.

Management of public health is devolved by the da Cunha Government with funding for the doctors and nurses provided by the UK Department for International Development (DFID). The DFID also funds visits from a number of clinical specialists throughout the year, including annual visits by dentists, dental technicians, and optometrists.

Primary health care doctors and narrow specialists are recruited from the entire world and assisted by the South Africa trained nurses and midwifes.

Current;y, the Government puts efforts to promote the preventive medicine instead of the curative health expenditures.

The 300 residents of the islands have public health insurance coverage for the emergency causes. Training courses for Basic Life Support are provided for every interested resident of the islands.

Below are some indices (from 2016) for the overall health profile of the archipelago:

Median age - 41.5 years
Gender ratio - 1.05 (M/F)
Life expectancy per birth - M 76.6 years, F 82.6 years
Neonatal mortality rate - 13.7/1000 live births
Total death rate - 7.7/1000 residents (i.e. 2.2 person per year).

Education

In the early days of Tristan's history, several of William Glass children were sent to England and South Africa for schooling. Occasional visitors were also asked to help teach island children.

The first teacher - Benjamin Pankhurst, arrived in 1830 for two years. Rev Taylor, Tristan's first minister, began a school, originally in William Glass' home, then in the largest Tristan house, built by Andrew Hagan which served as both church and school until 1923. This house, still a Hagan home, was one of the last remaining houses thatched with New Zealand Flax when pictured (left) in the 1980s.

During World War II, an expanded school was provided by the Naval Station and a new school house was built.

The Hagan Home

The present school, St. Mary, was built in 1975. It has five classrooms, a library, a hall with stage, a computer suite, a cookery room, and

St. Mary's School

45

craft/science room. St Mary's School educates Tristan children between the ages of three and sixteen.

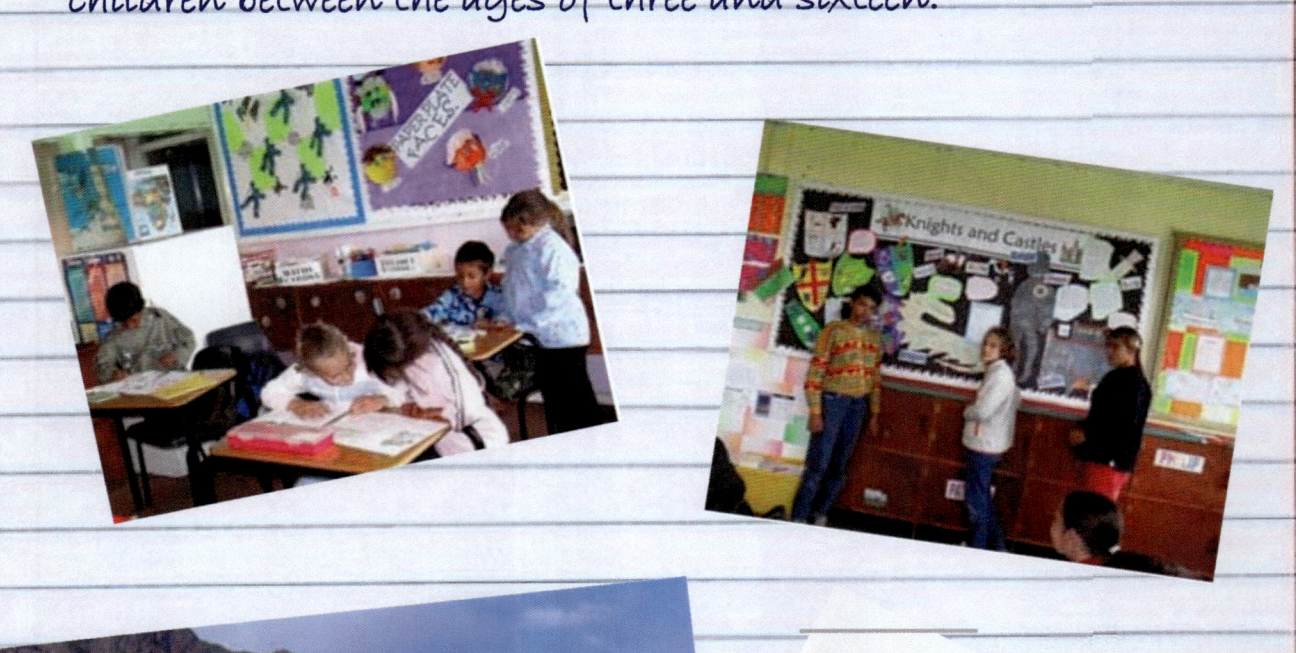

Crime

Come on! Really?

Do you genuinely believe, that in a place occupied by some 270-300 residents, where everyone is on display, where people know each other by heart, by flesh and by name, it would be easy to commit a crime? Perhaps some petty theft or DUI, but nothing harder.

Crime is almost non-existent on Tristan da Cunha. Doors remain unlocked. As the local patrols identify, when there are problems, they tend to come from the yachters and tourists.

There is one full-time police officer and three special constables for the four islands. There is one prison, in St. Helena, the smallest prison in the world.

"Last time we used our holding cell was back in the 70s, before I was a policeman, when there was a knife fight on a fishing vessel," says a local policeman.

"Today, we only have one bunk, there's no washing facilities and the door is made of plywood so it wouldn't take a strong man to break it down," continues the police officer who can't wait to retire at his age of 48 years.

The one and only Police Station and Correction Bunk, Edinburgh

Packing back

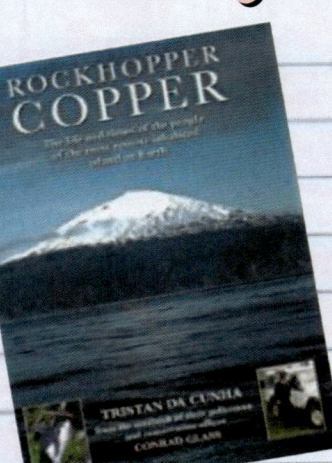

I found this book at Tristan's Post Office. Entitled "Rockhopper Copper" (2005), it is written by Conrad Glass, Tristan da Cunha's longtime Police and Conservation officer. It's the first book about this archipelago, written by an Islander. It'll entertain my soporific journey back to Montana.

I turned the first pages and met something that I need to share with you. I quote Conrad:

"To the people of Tristan da Cunha: be steadfast to your livelihood. For in it, you have a unique God-given lifestyle of unprecedented freedom over your destiny, that many people envy but may never have."

I can't agree more. The Tristanians master the art of isolation for a good reason. In today's geopolitical heyday, the complete concealment in the midst of the south Atlantic, where the Rockhopper penguins are de rigueur, is perhaps the best method for keeping the mind and spirit unaltered.

Yet, I have to say so-long to my Rockhopper friend! You are undoubtedly charming, and leaving you is uneasy. But I have a girlfriend, Phineloppe, waiting for me in Montana.

Printed in Great Britain
by Amazon